PRAISE FOR BURHAN AL-DIN FILI'S
THE SPECTACULAR ESCAPE

"In the oppressive shadows of communism, a humble Albanian couple discovers a path to a fresh start. How do they achieve this? Through a meticulously plotted, clandestine, and audacious escape. Fili graciously shares a concise tale that conveys a profound message: never waver in faith, and always harbor courage and hope, even when confronted with overwhelming adversity. By uplifting friends, family, and neighbors, we elevate ourselves."

—**Brandon Mayfield**, author of *Atheism Versus Belief*

"Well written, insightful, and inspiring... Mr. Fili knows best how to share a story and connect to the reader through his gift of words and expression...This is a story of faith, patience, and gratitude you won't ever forget!"

—*Crescent Reviews*

"A beautiful story to inspire you and the generations to come… As seen in his previous work, Fili is a master storyteller and you will get a feel for this as he walks you through this real-life narrative full of struggle, hope and light…Highly recommended."

—**Flamur Vehapi**, author of *Kosovo: A Brief Chronology* and *Verses of the Heart*

"Yet again Mr. Fili introduces us to an extraordinary story of noble endeavor, conviction, and hope for all of those seeking a daily dose of inspiration…I cannot recommend it enough!"

—**Naser Bresa**, professor, and author of *Retrospektiva*

THE SPECTACULAR ESCAPE

A True Story

BURHAN AL-DIN SEJDI FILI

Crescent Books

Crescent Books

Copyright © 2023 by Burhan Al-Din Fili
First Published in December 2023
by Crescent Books
an imprint of Crescent Institute LLC
Portland, OR.
e-mail: crescent.books2020@gmail.com
All rights reserved. No part of this publication
may be reproduced, stored in any retrieval system,
or transmitted, in any form or by any means, electronic,
mechanical, photocopying, recording or otherwise
without prior written permission from the publisher.

Translated from Albanian by
Ermira Pashaj
Prepared and typeset
by Elipse Productions
Paperback
ISBN: 978-1-954935-05-1
Subjects:
Story | Faith | Escape
Poems | Inspirations
Islam
First English edition.
Includes biographical references and appendices
Text copy edited by Stella Williams

Cover design by Elipse Productions
Printed in the United States of America

*These are the words of Burhan,
from Koplik a handful of soil,
love for Islam and his country
burns him like a candle's oil.*

WITH GRATITUDE

I express my sincere thanks and appreciation to the Alsar Foundation (Fondacioni Alsar), a very popular entity throughout the Albanian territories, for its outstanding contributions to all facets of cultural and artistic life, particularly with its unique publications that are helpful to Albanian readers. One of their many contributions is the publication of this story in Albanian. For this, I would especially like to thank the chairman of Alsar, Mr. Mehdi Gurra, who has always been and continues to be a promoter and initiator of introducing readers to high-quality work and publications in classical and contemporary topics, especially the historical ones I personally enjoy. I wish the Alsar team continued success in their selfless endeavors to spread cultural and Islamic values to Albanian Muslims around the world. Let their efforts serve as a model for others to follow!

Burhan Al-Din Fili,
USA & Albania, 2023

CONTENTS

With gratitude	7
When the impossible becomes possible	11
Dedication	15
A note from the author	17
Communism in Albania	21
The establishment of cooperatives	22
Unshakable belief in Allah	26
Conquering fear is the greatest victory in the world	28
Decision to escape	29
Preparations for the construction of the boat	31
An unexpected surprise	36
Reaching the lake	38

The epic role of the children	41
Arrival on the western shore of Lake Shkodra, Montenegro	45
The beginning of a new life	47
Emigration of the eldest boys to America	48
The rest of the family reunites in America	50
How I knew Qazim and the others	52
The Devotion of the Believer	56
Michigan	57
Glossary of terms, names, and places	58
Appendix B:	61
The Albanian Alphabet and Transliteration Chart	60
Appendix C:	65
A Timeline of Albania and the Region	64
About author	71
Ather titles by crescent books	72

BURHAN AL-DIN SEJDI FILI

WHEN THE IMPOSSIBLE BECOMES POSSIBLE

Building a boat was like wringing water from a stone.
But Qazim was pretty much determined:
"That is something to be done!"

As if everything against them said its word:
"That is something you cannot afford.
Don't you see? Don't you comprehend?
Such decisions are a great mistake."
"Don't even consider that orchestration.
Don't put your family in a tough situation!"

Voices like these and so many more,
were as if written on the shore.
But Qazim and Zoja had no fear;
They turned a deaf ear.

THE SPECTACULAR ESCAPE: A TRUE STORY

They had a strong conviction,
And by their side was God's benediction.
To open so many doors in your life,
You should be ready to sacrifice.
A true man never breaks his word!

So, without any hesitation,
They started the work for their salvation.
The whole family was invited,
Starting with "*Bismilah*" and united.
They worked with wisdom and in disguise,
to protect their work from doubting eyes.[1]

The neighbors would pass nearby,
having no idea what was going on.
Giving thanks to Almighty God.
The boat was almost built.

Qazim and Zoja were so pleased,
to see and caress that masterpiece.
The masterpiece of the big break,

---

[1] See *Glossary of Terms, Names, and Places* at the end of this book.

Which would carry them across the lake.
What a magnificent state!
When His help leads you to the gate!
Divine Wisdom, it is called,
Neither bought, nor sold,
Many blessings are yet to unfold.

Qazim and Zoja had such self-assurance.
They knew no fear or distress.
Working with joy and delight,
In the darkness, finding light.
A beacon to the pursuer,
A dazzling flash to the cruel.

In that difficult new start
Allah was always in their hearts.
Their descendants did the same.
Leading their lives in His Name.

I dedicate these words to remember these people,
whose brevity makes it difficult to find their equal.

DEDICATION

This book is dedicated to Qazim and Zoja Beci and their children, those silent heroes who conquered their fear and led their way to a free world. May Allah bless them in this world and the next.

A NOTE FROM THE AUTHOR

The communist regime, which was imposed upon the Albanian people, overcame them at the end of 1944. The Communist Party of the former Yugoslavia, with Tito as its leader, installed the communist regime via dishonest methods and by exercising violence. Enver Hoxha and his associates were only servants—followers of Tito and his tactics—who were supported by ominous international forces with evil intentions.

The introduction of communism in Albania resulted in isolation and a dimming of the people's lives, and they did not think this system would last for a long time.[2] Albanians were naive when it came to this. Indeed, they were never interested in the communist system, since it went against who they were as people connected to God.

---

[2] See *Appendix C* at the end of this book.

THE STORY

Communism in Albania

In 1948, Albania cut off its ties with Titoism, at least in appearance. This regime continued to conduct politics with diplomacy, giving its people limited liberties while very helpfully leaving their vassal leader, Enver Hoxha, to act with his people as a reserve. Albania became a desert island as a result of the breakup with Yugoslavia. In this situation, our people were forced to endure unrelenting misery with no assistance from anyone. Nobody cared about the Albanian people, their neighbors in particular.[3]

The populace started to realize that fleabag partisans weren't just a joke but a reality that overtook their lives. The bonds of captivity were very heavy, and the people were left speechless, as they did not know what to say or to whom to complain.

The communist regime began its cruel experiment following the directives of Stalin, which were brought to life with atheistic fanaticism; for the Albanian people, these were foreign concepts. But who could dare refuse them?

---

[3] See *Appendix B* at the end of this book.

The establishment of cooperatives (collectivization)

Collectivization started in the 1950s, a practice that was not just unknown, but also unimaginable to our people, who were accustomed to living according to their centuries-old traditional values.

The extortion of private property and the formation of the *kolkoze* are forms of material and social slavery that lead to idleness and the impoverishment of families and society as a whole. Collectivization of private property 'willingly,' as the Soviet system called it, pins man to its yoke in the absence of freedom with which he naturally lives. This freedom is a shelter that preserves the values of privacy, which are more than necessary to lead a normal life.

Private property is sacred; it cannot be taken advantage of, much less extorted in the name of 'voluntary collectivization'! Joining the cooperative is similar to becoming a member of a flock of sheep entering the sheepfold. The shepherd orders them to go in and out, feeds them, and milks them… whenever the shepherd wants. The purpose of communalism is to collectivize people in every action, thought, approach, and walk of life… It leads to social deprivation by killing every good thing for the sake of an aimless and frozen collective. This facilitated the undermining work of the notorious State Security, which permeated every stigma of society by sowing fear and terror. The 'New Man' product was delivered as a result. Naturally, from this hybrid man, we cannot expect any initiative for change; he is in a constantly torpid state.

Communist directives made people enter the 'collective fold'—'willingly,' or by violent means. There were those who understood and opposed, but without any means for recourse, because unfortunately, Albania turned into an 'experimental garden.'

One of many who opposed the directives was Sadik Zeka from Koplik. When the delegate from Tirana and Shkodra came to implement collectivization, Sadik Zeka resisted them openly, which made the delegate from Tirana show his anger like a petrifying beast. Sadik's father, who was an experienced man and as sharp as a tack, addressed the delegate: "Sir,"—the communist term 'friend' for addressing others had not yet entered the dictionary of collectivization that was being served with insistence—"this collectivism which you are talking about, is it done willingly or forcefully?"

The delegate felt somehow relieved and, in a self-important manner, said, "Uncle, for people like you who are able 'to understand,' it is done willingly; as for your son and his mates, it is done forcefully." "I understand," said the old man, while giving his son a reproachful look. Then he nodded and said, "Add my name to the list." And the job was finished. The delegates felt triumphant for their victory, for making people obey 'willingly,' something the old man and his friends were aware of, but who could dare do otherwise? In times of desperation, you call a pig uncle.

There were many like Sadik Zeka, whose voices and initiatives were made silent by invisible shackles. But Qazim Beci, who we will get to know shortly, took a different approach.

The policies of these strongmen knew no mercy or limit, worsening the Albanians' lives. People noticed the trap in which they had been caught. Only opportunists and subservient people who wanted to take advantage of the circumstances joined the administration.

People began to consider how they could escape their predicament. How they could take another path, quietly, to find a way out of this fold. The chances of survival were few and dangerous, and any delay would make it difficult to get out of there. However, there were some who refused to give in and were prepared to sacrifice everything for the best gift Allah has given man: freedom. Hence, nothing should be spared for it.

One of them was Qazim Beci (Xhilaj), with the help of his wife, Zoja. They were from the village of Sterbeq Buze Uji, Koplik (of Shkodra).

Qazim was about forty, and had five children with Zoja; the oldest was 14 years old, and Zoja was pregnant with their sixth child. Qazim was a hardworking man and a highly respected one, in particular by the *imam*, Iljaz Hoxha. These traits showed his unwavering devotion to Allah, which he had been demonstrating in all aspects of his life.[4]

---

[4] See *Appendix B* at the end of this book.

THE SPECTACULAR ESCAPE: A TRUE STORY

Unshakable belief in Allah

Qazim and Zoja were true believers with a strong faith, and the society that loved and respected them was their witness. They were fully aware that the communist system was cruel toward people and did not spare anything or anyone it encountered. The vision of this couple was rooted in their faith in Allah, against Whom the communists had declared war.

Qazim and Zoja concluded that the only way to save themselves from these faithless fools was to escape. But the question arose: 'How could this dangerous orchestration be realized?' They now had six children, the eldest being 14 and the youngest a newborn… The neighbors were very close, the lake was very vast; everything seemed to be to their disadvantage.

It was in 1958 when Qazim and Zoja pondered how they could manage this complicated and almost unattainable plan. But for Qazim and Zoja, nothing was unreachable. The firm belief they had in Allah gave them courage, strength, foresight, and steadfastness in every step of life—a life devoted to the service of Allah. How could they trust their lives to the communists? Qazim and Zoja, having a strong faith in Allah, would wring water from stone to chase their dream. This came from the awareness that both had cultivated in the world of *iman* with humility.

Our Prophet ﷺ said: «Humility is my pride."

This was the radiance of the teachings of Imam Iljaz Hoxha, whom they loved and followed, and he loved them as a teacher loves his students. An honest and open relationship between the imam and the *jamah* creates a beautiful and fruitful environment.

Their conviction to take this self-sacrificing path showed the harmony and love between one another. This spirit of cooperation helped them reconcile their decision to escape. It was a big, and dangerous decision, full of sacrifices.

Conquering fear is the greatest victory in the world

Who can make such decisions except those who have overcome their fear?

The decision to escape was made, but the question arose: How? The house of Qazim was closer to the lake than the other houses. In Sterbeq there is the vastest area of Shkodra's Lake. The escape could only be made by boat.

Where could they find one? There was only one boat that Ahmet Oso owned—a fisherman and fellow villager who had official permission to fish. Qazim could never accept plundering his boat in order to achieve his own objective, the journey to freedom.

Zoja and Qazim discussed this topic seriously for many hours. The only option for the six-child family was to construct their own watercraft inside their home. How could they persuade their children to remain silent during the time that they would be building the boat? Such a frightening decision needs great faith, but these parents had raised such children, which is hard to believe…

Decision to escape

Qazim and Zoja decided with confidence, conviction, courage, and determination to make preparations for the construction of the boat. The first thing they did was convince their children to keep it a secret and lend a hand when it was needed. They successfully achieved this. Their education was not casual work but a long process that produced wonderful results.

They needed a well-studied plan to build the boat, and there was no room for errors. They could finish the project with all the tools they needed the following year, especially the oxen and the cart, which they needed to pull the boat near the lakefront. Qazim would build the boat inside his house with the help of his family, who were ready to do whatever was asked of them...

Another important thing he needed was official permission to work privately. Qazim was the last one to enter the cooperative, and occasionally local governmental bodies reminded him not to delay. Shrewdly, he always expressed his willingness to join the collective, and since some of his friends were Communist Party members, they tolerated his postponement. Not all members of the party had communist convictions, and as such, they helped people whenever it was possible. Like in Qazim's case, who asked to be allowed to take the products of that year, given the large family he had.

Thankfully this time, the local government granted him the permission he needed to work privately until the end of the autumn. That was all Qazim and Zoja needed.

Preparations for the construction of the boat

Preparing the groundwork for the construction of the rowboat was a hard, difficult job that required courage, patience, and skill. These traits were present in Qazim, but not necessarily for boat building, which is an art in itself. Even so, he had such confidence that nothing could stop him.

The large family required extra space, so they decided to build a room. They told friends about their plan to spread the word about the work at home. Some of them assisted in laying the foundations, a job that was traditionally done voluntarily and contributed to improving social ties. He thanked them for their help and remarked, "Concerning the rest of the work, I will do it slowly, *insha'Allah*."

He collected all the necessary materials, like stones, boards, cement, and tar, and told friends he would cover it with roof decking; that's why he needed tar. He purchased all the materials in Shkodra, which he carried home in his ox-drawn cart.

He chose the planks carefully so they could be suitable for the construction of the legendary boat. He was very skilled and could do all the work needed in housebuilding.

He could do the work of a stonemason, carpenter, etc., but he was not skilled at boatbuilding—again, an entirely different art in itself.

Nothing could stop the will and support of Zoja and the children. Qazim began to build the walls and later isolated the roof deck with tar. He left some of it in order to isolate the boat planks, which he would build in the most cleverly secretive manner. The whole family participated in accordance with their individual tasks. To work on the construction of the rowboat without being noticed, another loud noise had to be created to silence the blows and carving sounds while working on the boat. It was time when the wheat was ripe, so Zoja harvested some, telling her neighbors that they had run out of flour and needed to harvest the wheat…

On one side, Qazim started with wood cutting and carving; on the other side, Zoja and her elder sons, Maliq and Haxhia, were hitting the wheat with very big sticks in order to thresh it. It was a traditional method to separate the seeds from the chaff until the threshing machine was introduced. So, this way they camouflaged the noise during this holy endeavor, which, with God's help, would be their salvation. As they were working, the third son, Ahmet, was keeping watch around the house, looking for possible visitors... Whereas Sadija, their only daughter, was taking care of her little brothers, Skender and baby Xhevdet, the little darling, whose angelic silence was a much needed blessing during those difficult days. *SubhanAllah*!

The family continued to work on this legendary mission with mastery, care, and hope.

Meanwhile, the boat of Ahmet Oso was occasionally brought to the shore of the lake, where it was anchored near a very dense forest. Qazim would go there often and carefully study the construction of the boat, while trying to measure its length, width, depth, the bowing of the planks, as well as the boat's front and back. He was trying to figure out how deep the boat had to stay in the water when it was empty and loaded. He studied all this with attention and coolness, because no one had any idea about his plan. Such a study helped Qazim continue his spectacular work. He often used to draw small sketches to be more focused on this family work. Working on the boat and the children's engagement were in accordance with one another and left no room for any doubt.

Qazim would also occasionally meet his neighbors, with whom he had honest relations, be they Muslims or Catholics.

THE SPECTACULAR ESCAPE: A TRUE STORY

While Qazim was building the boat, he studied the terrain and movements of people, especially the border patrol, who passed by his house because it was closest to the lake. The soldiers patrolling the border passed through the Kamica border post, a few kilometers north of Qazim's village. Soldiers often stopped by his house, where they found the generosity of Qazim Beci; he would give them fruit according to season, as well as food on occasion. During the winter he would shelter them from the cold and heavy rain, and occasionally they would have a nap...

Qazim noticed that the motorboat patrolling the lake from Zogaj village up to Kamica had not been seen recently. In a casual way, he asked them about it. They responded that the motorboat had a technical issue and had been sent to Tirana to get repaired, which would take a very long time. So fortunately, it was on Qazim's side to finish his work. Qazim was always one step ahead of the State Security, and he skillfully overcame them with a strong and firm faith in Allah.

Qazim's activity inside the house was done carefully, though at a rapid pace. At that point, everything was going well. Under those circumstances, working on the boat was challenging and required patience and skill, traits that Qazim did not lack. His faithful and wise wife was a great support, as were the children, who were very focused and alert in keeping the secret.

Although their vigilance was at its peak, it was almost impossible to monitor the situation in every detail. Unexpectedly, something happened in the course of their activity…

An unexpected surprise

One day, while working, Qazim and the whole family were surprised by the unintended entry of Mark Lek Vata, their neighbor, who was a good and loyal friend. Mark's presence surprised the children, who were responsible for keeping watch.

When Qazim saw Mark, he was not shocked because he knew his loyalty was beyond reproach. Mark looked at Qazim and addressed him with words that expressed nobility: "No doubt, I am with you."

Mark was a master of carpentry. Both he and Qazim started working to finish the ship's construction as soon as possible. Mark kept the secret, like Qazim did. He told his wife, who expressed readiness for such a sacrifice. All this was a secret pact between them.

Qazim's children did not show any sign of discouragement, but rather felt safe when they saw the determination of their parents in that difficult situation. God has wisdom in everything; sometimes it appears that the worst has befallen you, but later you realize it is actually a benefit to you.

Qazim and Mark continued the work that brought about the completion of the boat, which looked good. Mark's presence would also be a great help when putting the boat into the cart, which would not be easy for Qazim and Zoja and their children, in such extreme and unimaginable conditions.

The night was approaching, and the trip on the homemade boat was ahead.

Reaching the lake

SubhanAllah! The faith, obedience, foresight, lonesomeness, and self-sacrifice of two noble spouses, Qazim and Zoja, helped by their children, were confounded with the completion of the construction of the boat, in which the faithful neighbor became part of that magnificent project. May God honor them all.

It was decided that the boat launch on the lake should be held on the night of the Assembly, which was held from time to time, a kind of organizational activity that our people were not used to. It was a Communist habit, a disorienting and destructive one, to which Qazim had declared war: a kind of *jihad* in his own way.

The gathering took place far from Qazim's house, at the commencement of the village. It went on for a very long time and featured nonsense speeches delivered by delegates from Tirana and Shkodra. Participation was mandatory, which made the launching steps easier. Qazim and Mark had decided to inform Mark's noble father, Leke—who was worried about his son because of what he had done—that as they got close to the lake, he would go and let the Assembly know that Mark wasn't home.

Then Mark and the others walked silently towards the lake. The place from which the boat would be pulled was a thin layer of wall, which facilitated the removal of the curtain wall and the loading of the boat onto the cart. The boat was not very heavy since it hadn't entered water before, which swells the planks and might cause problems after entering the lake.

It seemed that everything was in complete harmony for the realization of this almost unbelievable project; even the baby did not cry, as if he didn't exist at all: a divine miracle that helped achieve their spectacular goal.

Since the lake was very close, they did not delay and arrived at the shore. Without wasting time, they released the boat into the water, which began to suck water like a thirsty being, and not surprisingly, the water began to penetrate the gap between the planks, as the tar did not seem to do its job well. It was the quick intervention of the older children, who acted instinctively to remove the water...

They started to get on the boat; this was a somewhat unbearable sight for Mark's wife, who panicked and refused to board with her children on the boat. This created a difficult and dangerous situation that was necessary to resolve quickly and in a very calm way. Mark decided to return, but Qazim was determined to travel towards the destination God had oriented him towards: war against fear, march to victory. He told Mark to help him remove the water from the boat, which was heavy and loaded with materials, most of which ultimately had to be left on the shore.

BURHAN AL-DIN SEJDI FILI

The epic role of the children

Qazim's children continually bailed out water from the boat with small water containers. The children played a crucial role. Mark stayed on the shore while Qazim said goodbye to him and his homeland, which he never forgot. So Qazim said goodbye to Albania and his only sister, Zyba, who was married in Kalldrun, not far from Sterbeq.

Hafeedh Sabri Koçi told me a very interesting story about Qazim's sister when we were at an Islamic Conference in the 1990s, in Cairo. While conversing with the *hafeedh* until late hours at the hotel and strolling in the area, he told me about Qazim's sister, whose name he did not remember, and how she came to Koplik in 1945. It was a time when the hafeedh served as an imam in one of the mosques in Shkodra, when he was young. Although young in age, he had a good reputation, as he was an orator and quite charismatic, and the echo of his activity had spread to other areas.

Hafeedh Sabri continued to tell me how a lady from Koplik—Zyba, as it turned out—asked him to write a protective *hajmali* against every evil. She had given permission to her husband to marry another woman, hoping the second wife would give birth to a son. She had just one daughter, and if they had no sons, the husband's cousins would inherit the family property, leaving the girl without anything—according to the Canon,[5] but not according to Shari'a. Marriage to more than one wife was still allowed by the newly installed communist system, and agrarian reform was not yet established.

This interesting request surprised the hafeedh: "How can it happen that the wife herself finds a bride for her husband, and more than that, she goes herself to get her?" This was a new phenomenon for Albanian Muslims.

For Zyba's request, the hafeedh wrote something from the Qur'an, saying that everything is in God's hands, not our hands. She thanked him and went home cheerfully and full of hope. God blessed the young couple with three sons. Fadil was born in 1947, and later on, the new wife gave birth to Qemal and Nazim.

They called Zyba mother, whom they loved very much, and everything in the house was in her hands. I knew those three sons very well. They were brought up in a harmonious environment and with love and kindness. This was Zyba, the sister of Qazim Beci, the woman who made history. Hafeedh Sabri spoke of this event in such an emotional

---

[5] I.e. *The Kanun of Lekë Dukagjini* which is a set of Albanian traditional customary laws rooted in pagan and Christian beliefs from Roman and later Byzantine times.

way, as it had impressed him so much, despite the fact that it occurred more than fifty years ago.

As he told me about the event while we were walking on the Nile shore, I was trying to visualize the 'actors' of that story, whom I knew well. I cried out, "O Allah, this event should live in the people's memory; it cannot be forgotten…"

Qazim and his family started to row the oars as much as they could, and the boat, though a plain one, obeyed their strong and unbreakable will.

Meanwhile, Leke Vata, a true man, was reaching the place of the gathering (the Assembly), and when his sons and daughters-in-law saw him, they were stunned by his presence. He approached the leader, and with a half-drowned voice, he gave the news of Mark's departure with his family to the lake. Without letting Leke properly finish his announcement, the chairman was alarmed and gave orders to go to the lake. All communists and those who had weapons rushed towards the lake like jackals in search of prey.

Border posts in Kamice and the Interior Branch in Koplik were alerted. They would shoot rifles to show that they were able to arrest anyone who wanted to flee, but in reality, they didn't know anything yet…

It took them some time to reach the lake, and fortunately, Qazim's family had gotten so far across the lake by that point that no bullet could reach them, especially on that moonless night.

The noisy security forces were thundering self-assuredly onto the shore, and trying to tell anyone that nothing and nobody could escape, but Qazim and his family left them dumbstruck. Mark, who had been unable to leave, was arrested, but he never betrayed his friend, whom he helped. It had been a mission of help that would later be a heavy burden. This is life…!

Someone cries, and someone laughs. May God have mercy on Mark and all!

BURHAN AL-DIN SEJDI FILI

Arrival on the western shore of Lake Shkodra, Montenegro

Qazim continued to row with his family to the coast of freedom, which he unfortunately lacked in his homeland. But one's real homeland is Freedom.

On their way across the lake, they could only hear the noise of the small waves created by the movement of the boat as well as the sounds of oars struggling in the water. A long time had passed, and they kept looking at each other; no one talked.

It was a new day, in a new place, and in a new way, full of hope. They reached the shore, where some residents of the other side of the lake were surprised to see them. One of the residents informed the border forces, who came at once. When they saw the simple boat filled with people, they found it hard to believe that they had made it across the lake in that boat.

The family got off the boat one by one, and Zoja, with the baby on her arm, was aided by some of the residents. Everyone was tired, but full of hope. The police took them and moved towards Podgorica (called Titograd at that time).

Qazim and Zoja were questioned on how they dared get on that dreadful boat, and worst of all, with children inside. They were also asked about the reason for the escape.

They said, "We have come to seek freedom, not to harm anyone. We want to work hard to make a living." After some time, they freed them to go to Tuz, where Zoja's relatives lived, and where she herself was from.

They started a new life with people's help and their own efforts. The children adapted easily, speaking a little Albanian and a little Bosnian. Qazim, as the hardworking person and craftsman he was, started working daily, whenever it was possible. Soon he became a well-respected man. He started frequenting the mosque in Tuz. Zoja devoted herself to taking care of the house and the children, since it was a new environment and they needed their mother's presence. So, they settled in a new place, leading an honest and modest life, always with a firm and strong faith in God.

The beginning of a new life

Although it was a simple life, Qazim and Zoja did not let it become just another random life. With Qazim's hard labor and willingness to work, he left no room for demoralization, or despair. As he was a very skilled man, he could do whatever was needed in the environment of those days. He became a well-known and honored man. The children were grown up, and by that time another child came to life, a girl, the young child of the exemplary couple. The eldest son, Maliq, was married, since it was customary to marry at a young age.

While the other sons, Haxhia and Ahmet, continued school and at the same time worked different jobs. The little ones grew up under the care of the noble mother, who was a school of wisdom herself, educating great and noble humans.

Emigration of the eldest boys to America

In the mid-1960s, many Albanians from Albanian lands in former Yugoslavia began to emigrate, especially to America, the vast majority of whom were official Albanians. This Titist strategy aimed at reducing the Albanian population in our lands. But the large unemployment rate among Albanians also forced them to emigrate.

In this flood of migration, the three eldest sons of Qazim went to refugee camps in Italy. Not so long after that, they arrived in Detroit, Michigan, a state that had had an old and large presence of the Albanian community since the time of King Zog. This community had their own mosque; the imam, Vehbi Ismaili, was from Shkodra.

Haxhia and Ahmet started a new life in a world unknown to them. It was the first time they had been far away from family. It was like a skydiving jump, where you don't know where you are going. Emigration is difficult and dangerous if you are not capable of maneuvering in that complicated situation. Haxhia and Ahmet worked together to guard each other because it would be more dangerous without cooperation.

Shortly after that, the eldest brother, Maliq, who was married and had two children, departed for Italy. They took that perilous route through refugee camps. But trust in Allah is of crucial importance. Both Maliq and his brothers always successfully overcame the difficulties with devotion and reliance on God.

Their religious consciousness connected them with the Mosque and the Albanian imam, Vehbi Ismaili. They were very supportive of the Mosque and the imam.

The rest of the family reunites in America

While the three older sons of Qazim continued to live in America, he, his wife, and the four little children, who had already grown up, still lived in Tuz, without any prospects. This urged them to take the road to America and join their sons, who were already stabilized in Detroit. The family spent several months in Italy without any difficulty. Support from America facilitated their staying in that country.

Finally, it was time to reunite in a new place, far away from their homeland, but this union lightened the burden of emigration because the older boys, now grown men, were already stable in the United States.

Qazim wanted to see his children work and live together, but life changes, especially when you are an immigrant. The more the tree grows, the more its branches grow apart from each other.

Qazim began to adapt to his new life, despite his age. He began to frequent the Albanian Mosque and became friends with Imam Vehbi, who was almost his age. SubhanAllah!

In the late 1930s in Tirana's *Madrasa*, Imam Vehbi was a schoolmate of Iljaz Hoxha, who was known as the imam of Buze-Uji, a dear friend. And later, Iljaz's son, Xhevdet, became Qazim's son-in-law. Such family ties are only established by Allah!

Qazim and his family turned out to be the main supporters of Imam Vehbi and the mosque. They were by his side in every need.

THE SPECTACULAR ESCAPE: A TRUE STORY

How I knew Qazim and the others

In 1976, after I spent a month in prison in former Yugoslavia as a fugitive and later in a refugee camp in Italy, I arrived in Detroit, Michigan. There I met Qazim Beci and his sons, as well as his son-in-law, Xhevdet Hoxha, who was in fact the reason for us to meet and unite there in Detroit.

It was a warm meeting. We went to the house of Xhevdet, where we stayed for a week. His family welcomed us with generosity and a smile of hospitality. Xhevdet's help had been present since the days we were staying at the refugee camp in Italy.

By knowing everyone, I felt I was part of that family, embraced by the brothers' love and care. I started to get to know everyone closely, especially Qazim.

It was not the first time I had heard about Qazim. When he escaped in 1958, I was 9 years old. It was a hot summer morning, and I was staying with my father. At that moment, my uncle Cafi came and told my father, whispering in his ear, that Qazim Beci and his family had escaped using a boat… My father was astonished and entered deep thoughts in that troubled situation. As they were conversing, I started to imagine—like a child entering his pure world of imagination—escapes, boats, and a whole family running.

I was reminded of all this when I heard Qazim talking about the escape, and now we were reunited in a new place, far away from our homeland, Koplik.

I would often engage in meaningful and delightful conversations with Qazim and Zoja, which I still treasure in my memories.

Qazim, being a sharp-eyed and sharp-witted man, would often speak gently. During our visits, the tobacco smoke would drift smoothly in that hospitable environment. I felt like I was home. The kindness and compassion of the whole family embraced me, which I appreciated and preserved with love in my heart.

He continued his life with his family, which continued growing with the passing of time. They preserved their language and religion, and taught their children and grandchildren to walk on that path, albeit in exile. Qazim was active in helping the children, wherever and whenever it was needed. He learned to drive at the age of 60. To him, nothing was impossible…

He failed to learn English, but it did not prevent him from driving different routes. I was curious to know how he found the places he went. He used to tell me, "When I go somewhere, I try to remember certain places, buildings, and advertisements. I use them as orienting signs that help me get to the right place without any problems."

He used to go to the mosque, which was quite far away, but he would take secondary roads to avoid the highways. I asked him how he crossed the roads often with heavy traffic, and he would calmly tell me that he followed the traffic rules with strictness to not allow himself to be part of a possible accident. "I don't know who," he said, "but I'm afraid someone could crash into my car under the influence of alcohol or drugs."

Qazim and Zoja were enjoying the fruits of their noble work in raising and educating their children and grandchildren, who, *mashaAllah*, were in good health. But life sometimes surprises you with unexpected incidents. That's what happened to Qazim Beci, who died suddenly. Zoja and her children received this bad news with patience and faith, as it was God's will, and we must find peace and tranquility in the conviction that God never does evil.

Zoja lived many years after her husband passed away. She continued her life as if Qazim were alive, taking care of the family, which was her priority and main concern. The family cherished a strong faith and preserved God's *Amanah* by being devoted servants and always following the straight path. Zoja was able to see, educate, and give precious advice to her many grandchildren. You cannot easily find such Albanians who still practice their religion and speak their mother tongue. This is a true victory!

Every time I went to see them, Zoja eagerly awaited my arrival, and she would never allow me to go without inviting me to eat something. This way she communicated her kind world, which knew no limits, welcoming you with a carpet of generosity.

On a rainy day, now years later, with the Albanian imam, Shuajb Gërguri, I went to visit her in the hospital. She was tired but didn't give up. I said, "Be patient, Zoj, because with Allah's will, you will recover soon." She looked at me calmly, and with a sweet voice, she addressed me, "God never decrees evil."

Many years after that day, her words compelled me to write a poem about her and her strength, which taught me a great lesson.

THE SPECTACULAR ESCAPE: A TRUE STORY

The Devotion of the Believer

It was a day of constant rain,
I went to the hospital to visit her.
I walked in the door slowly,
And she greeted me with a smile, not words.

I sat slowly down by her,
With a whisper shared by get well wishes,
Then she looked at me with a beaming light
A soothing world, like that of a mother.

"Thankfully I am well and have no complaints,
The Gracious God does not do injustice!"
She said those words with a pleasing smile,
The pains she suffered she didn't view as a punishment,
Instead she bore them with faith and patience,
As if she were imparting on me an important lesson.

A few days later I went my way,
Then I learned of her saddening death.
A noble woman by name and presence
A courageous person whose likes are hard to find.

Michigan

After the hospital visit, we said goodbye, and we left. I never saw her again, but I never forgot her or her honorable husband, Qazim Beci. It never occurred to me, nor did I think, that one day I would write about them and their heroism. They were real *mujahids*; they never died. May God have mercy on them! May the gardens of Paradise be their dwelling place! Amen!

GLOSSARY OF TERMS, NAMES, AND PLACES

ﷺ: 'God's peace and blessings be upon him' (an honorific used after the name of Prophet Muhammad)

Albania: a country in the Balkan Peninsula (Southeastern Europe)

Allah: the Arabic term for 'God' used by Muslim and non-Muslim speakers of Arabic

Amanah: trust (the term encompasses all the religious duties of Islam)

Bismilah: (the Muslim formula to begin an action) with/ in the name of God

Enver Hoxha: the communist dictator of Albania (d. 1985)

Hafeedh: someone who has memorized the Quran; also often transliterated as 'hafez'

Hajmali: an amulet

Imam: religious (and often community) leader; leader of prayers

Insha'Allah: 'God willing' or 'if God wills it'

Islam: lit. submission to the will of God alone; the faith of the Muslim community

Jamah: congregation of Muslims

Jihad: a worthy struggle

Kolkoze: from Russian 'kolkhoz,' a Soviet farming cooperative

Madrasa: 'school'; in this context an Islamic school

MashaAllah: 'Praise be to God'; an expression of praise, gratitude, joy, and recognition

Mujahid: a person who struggles for a noble cause in God's path

Shkodra: old city in northern Albania

SubhanAllah: 'Glory be to God'

THE SPECTACULAR ESCAPE: A TRUE STORY

Fig. 1. Map of Albania. Map is public domain from Wikimedia Commons. Accessed in 2023.

APPENDIX B:

The Albanian Alphabet and Transliteration Chart

Letters	Read as	Pronounce	Albanian examples	English equivalent
A	a	a	a	afër	f<u>a</u>r
B	b	bë	b	bukë	<u>b</u>at
C	c	cë	ts	ceremoni	i<u>ts</u>y
Ç	ç	ë	tʃ	çelës	<u>ch</u>at
D	d	dë	d	dasëm	<u>d</u>oor
Dh	dh	dhë	ð	dhelpër	<u>th</u>ere
E	e	e	e	emër	<u>e</u>nter
Ë	ë	ë	ə	ëmbël	<u>a</u>round

Letters	Read as	Pronounce	Albanian examples	English equivalent
F	f	fë	f	fletë	fly
G	g	gë	g	gurë	gum
Gj	gj	gjë	ɟ	gjeneral	join
H	h	hë	h	hap	hat
I	i	i	i	interes	sea
J	j	jë	j	javë	yawn
K	k	kë	k	këmishë	kite
L	l	lë	l	lopë	leave
Ll	ll	llë	ł or l	llampë	mill
M	m	më	m	mal	man
N	n	në	n	nënë	no

Letters	Read as	Pronounce	Albanian examples	English equivalent
Nj	nj	një	ɲ	njeri	o<u>ni</u>on
O	o	o	o	orë	<u>o</u>pen
P	p	pë	p	parti	<u>p</u>en
Q	q	që	q	qumësht	ma<u>t</u>ure
R	r	rë	ɾ	raport	<u>r</u>ed
Rr	rr	rrë	r (rolled)	rrjesht	*bo<u>rr</u>ow
S	s	së	s	stacion	<u>s</u>top
Sh	sh	shë	ʃ	shtëpi	<u>sh</u>op
T	t	të	t	telefon	<u>t</u>ree
Th	th	thë	θ	thupër	<u>th</u>in

THE SPECTACULAR ESCAPE: A TRUE STORY

Letters	Read as	Pronounce	Albanian examples	English equivalent
U	u	u	u	urë	f<u>oo</u>d
V	v	vë	v	vezë	<u>v</u>est
X	x	xë	dz	xixë	ad<u>ze</u>
Xh	xh	xhë	dʒ	xhaxha	<u>J</u>upiter
Y	y	y	y	yll	*n<u>ew</u>
Z	z	z	z	zemër	<u>z</u>ebra
Zh	zh	zhë	ʒ	zhurmë	plea<u>s</u>ure

*No exact English equivalent is found. Equivalent to *mons<u>ieu</u>r* in French.[6]

---

[6] This chart is from *Kosovo: A Brief Chronology* by Flamur Vehapi.

APPENDIX C:[7]

A Timeline of Albania and the Region

168 BCE: The region of Illyria is conquered by the Romans

547 CE: The first Slavic invasions of the region begin

850s CE: Kosova is absorbed by the Bulgarian Empire

1018 CE: The region becomes part of Byzantium

1300s: Serbian principality of Rascia conquers Kosova. This period witnesses the building of Serbian Orthodox churches and monasteries across Kosova

1389: The armies of the Balkans (Serbs, Albanians, Bosnians, and others) under King Lazar are defeated at the Battle of Kosova (the Field of Blackbirds) by the Ottoman armies under the rule of Sultan Murad I

1443: Skanderbeg rebels against the Ottomans

1448: The Second Battle of Kosova consolidates Ottoman rule in the Balkans

---

[7] This appendix is from *Kosovo: A Brief Chronology* by Flamur Vehapi.

THE SPECTACULAR ESCAPE: A TRUE STORY

1453: Sultan Mehmed (Muhammad) Fatih conquers Constantinople (names it Istanbul); Albania and Kosova come under Ottoman control

1467: The Albanian Kingdom comes under direct control of the Ottomans, enjoying internal autonomy

1521: Sultan Suleyman the Magnificent conquers Belgrade (the capital of Serbia)

1600-1700: The majority of Albanians willingly convert to Islam

1877-1878: The Ottoman Empire loses its foothold in Serbia, Montenegro and Bulgaria due to the Russo-Ottoman war

1912: The First Balkan War; Albania declares independence from the Ottomans; Serbs occupy Kosova

1913: Kosova is incorporated into the Kingdom of Serbia

1928: Ahmed Bey Zogu, after being president of Albania for several years with support from Yugoslavia, becomes King Zog I

1937: Serbian Vaso Čubrilović writes the secret memorandum 'Expulsion of Albanians' advocating for a forced removal of all Albanians from Kosova (who at this point are around 90% Muslim)

1939: Italy invades Albania

1941: Josip Tito organizes the partisan movement in Yugoslavia; Kosova becomes part of the Italian-controlled Albania; Enver Hoxha takes lead of the Communist Party

1943: Germany invades Albania

1944: Communists in Albania establish provisional government and appoint Enver Hoxha as Prime Minister

1945: Churchill gives Kosova, Macedonia, Slovenia and Croatia to Communist Yugoslavia under the rule of Tito; religious communities suffer a reign of terror

1945-1951: Thousands of Kosovar Albanians are murdered and expelled to Turkey after being labeled as 'Turks' due to their shared faith with the Turks

1946: Kosova is absorbed into the Yugoslav federation; Socialist People's Republic of Albania is proclaimed

1948: Tito breaks with USSR

1961: Albania allies itself with China

1968: First demonstrations for the independence of Kosova take place; many are arrested

1974: The Yugoslav constitution declares Kosova an Autonomous Province of Yugoslavia

1980: Yugoslav leader Tito dies; Serbs begin their campaign to retake Kosova from Albanians and make it a province of 'Greater Serbia'

1985: Enver Hoxha dies

1991: The Yugoslav Federation is dissolved; the European Community establishes an Arbitration Commission to make decisions regarding recognition of its former constituents as independent countries. This Commission accepts Slovenia's and Croatia's applications, but not that of Bosnia or Kosova

1992: Albania's Democratic Party wins elections, and Salih Berisha becomes president. In Kosova, Ibrahim Rugova, an advocate of non-violence, is elected the first president of the Republic of Kosova; Bosnia holds its referendum and 99% of the ballots come in favor of independence. (However, at the time, the Serbs were preparing for a slaughter of the Bosnian Muslims)

1992-5: Serbian extremists carry out genocide in Bosnia. In July of 1995, two years after being declared a 'Safe Haven' by the UN, over 8000 Bosnian Muslims are massacred in Srebrenica

1996-7: Hate-filled Serb nationalist, Vojislav Šešelj, publicly advocates infecting Kosovar Albanians with the AIDS virus; Kosova Liberation Army (KLA) emerges as a reaction to the Serbian barbarous regime throughout Kosova

1997: Unrest in Albania brings the Socialists to power; Serbian military offensive increases tremendously in Kosova; U.S. and E.U. diplomats are repeatedly deceived by Milošević's false promises to end his campaign of ethnic cleansing in Kosova

1999: In June, NATO's 72-day airstrike campaign ends the Serbian occupation of Kosova; UN Security Council passes the Security Council Resolution 1244 placing Kosova under transitional UN administration (UNMIK)

2003: The Socialist Party wins in Albania

2008: On February 17, Kosova declares independence, but Serbia rejects it, calling it illegal under international law; in April, Kosova's parliament adopts new constitution; in December, European Union mission (Eulex) takes over police, justice and customs services from UN in Kosova

2009: Albania joins NATO

ABOUT AUTHOR

Burhan Al-Din Fili was born in Koplik, Albania, which at the time was under the Communist regime that strangled the country for decades. Young Burhan, however, refused to be cowed by an atheist regime. In 1976 he swam across Lake Shkodra, reaching former Yugoslavia where he was caught, jailed and interrogated. Later, he escaped to Italy where he lived in a refugee camp. In 1977 he moved to the United States, and in 1982 Fili went to Egypt where he studied Arabic and Islamic Studies at the renowned Al-Azhar University. After the collapse of Communism in 1991, he returned to Albania where he contributed to the democratic life of his people. When the regime of Milošević viciously attacked Kosova in 1999, Fili joined Mercy USA, a humanitarian organization, in order to help the refugees there. To this day he contributes to helping the needy in different parts of the world. Fili is married and has four children.

OTHER TITLES BY CRESCENT BOOKS

Atheism Versus Belief by Brandon Mayfield, 2023

Kosovo: A Brief Chronology by Flamur Vehapi, 2023

Verses of the Heart: Poems by Flamur Vehapi, 2021

Ertugrul Ghazi: A Very Short Biography by Flamur Vehapi, 2021

BURHAN AL-DIN SEJDI FILI

What I wrote, I will leave behind me
let it be read by whoever pleases to do so;
for show-off I wont take a single step,
because only Allah knows me best.

www.ingramcontent.com/pod-product-compliance
Lightning Source LLC
Chambersburg PA
CBHW031419040426
42444CB00005B/645